anythink

D0576345

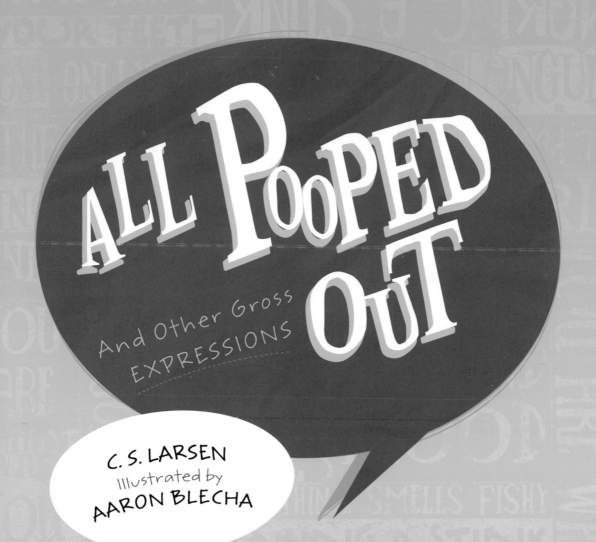

ALL POOPED OUT

And Other Gross EXPRESSIONS

C. S. LARSEN

Illustrated by

AARON BLECHA

Lerner Publications Company

MINNEAPOLIS

To Mom and Dad, who helped control the farting
around when I was all pooped out.

Special thanks to my editor, Sara Hoffmann, as I
sweated blood from looming deadlines.

Lerner Publications Company
A division of Lerner Publishing Group, Inc.
241 First Avenue North
Minneapolis, MN 55401 U.S.A.

Website address: www.lernerbooks.com

Library of Congress Cataloging-in-Publication Data

Larsen, C. S. (Christopher Sterling), 1966–
    All pooped out and other gross expressions /
  by. C. S. Larsen.
       p.   cm. — (It's just an expression)
    Includes index.
    ISBN 978-0-7613-7892-1 (lib. bdg. : alk. paper)
    1. English language—Idioms—Juvenile literature.
  I. Title.
  PE1460.L36 2013
  428.1—dc23   2011036216

Manufactured in the United States of America
1 – PC – 7/15/12

TABLE of CONTENTS

INTRODUCTION

So you're in the library, **all pooped out** from a long day of school, **sweating blood** about the history project that's due tomorrow. You don't want to **make a big stink** about it, but you'll be lucky if you meet the project's deadline **by the skin of your teeth.** What's that smell? Did somebody pass gas over in the science section? Probably some **snot-nosed brat farting around.** Yuck! You think **you're gonna hurl.**

What's with sweating blood, making a stink, and farting around? Sounds confusing—and gross. Well, these phrases are all idioms. Idioms are sayings that mean something different from what you might think they mean. But don't get your undies in a bunch. Once you discover what folks are *really* saying when they use idioms, the phrases suddenly won't seem so mysterious. And soon you'll be using them like a pro! Just don't **bite your tongue** while doing so, because you know what they say: **you are what you eat.**

SWEATING BLOOD

Olivia's sweating blood over her spelling test. Wow! Olivia sounds like she's in big trouble. Is she OK? Is blood actually oozing from her body?

Of course not. ***Sweating blood* just means she's really stressed out by the tough test.** It's an expression you say when you're stuck with a challenging thing to do.

So where does the expression come from? What does sweating blood have to do with difficult tasks? It turns out that it comes from the fact that people actually *have* sweated blood when they were stressed out. No kidding!

The scientific term for sweating blood is hematidrosis. It can happen when a person is facing an extremely high-pressure situation. Your heart beats rapidly, and your blood pumps superfast.

Will *you* spring a leak the next time you feel stressed? Probably not. Hematidrosis is incredibly rare. But just reading about it kind of makes you want to be more prepared for your next spelling test, doesn't it?

This girl's in full-on freak-out mode about her spelling test. You might say she's sweating blood.

I'M GONNA HURL!

Eric just ate a bowl of broccoli, and now he says he's gonna hurl.

There are lots of ways to hurl things, but Eric's talking about the big V—vomit. Yep. This hurling is all about emptying the contents of your stomach. **That's what people mean when they say they're gonna hurl.**

The technical term for hurling is emesis. It happens when your stomach muscles contract, sending whatever's in your stomach out of your mouth and (hopefully) into a toilet. (Better there than on your math homework—although hurling *would* be a pretty good excuse for not making it through those multiplication problems.)

Fresh broccoli can be super delicious...no, really! But eating a food that you just don't like can make you feel like you're gonna hurl.

People usually hurl when they have a stomach illness, eat rotted food, or take a ride in a rocking boat or a jostling car. It's the body's way of quickly getting rid of food that the stomach's too upset to digest. It can also protect you from letting bad stuff get in your system, which could make you *really* sick.

Hurling is never fun—but just remember that everyone does it. The next time it happens to you, try to stay calm. Then lie down or sit down for a while. Try sipping a little water once your stomach settles down. The good news is that you'll probably feel a lot better after you hurl.

Ugh—that "gonna hurl" feeling is no fun at all.

FARTING AROUND

Dillon and Tyrone got together after school to quiz each other for their big science test. But Dillon just couldn't seem to settle down. First, he started making paper airplanes out of flash cards. Then he set the science books up like goalposts and tore a corner off a worksheet to make a soccer ball. When he flicked the makeshift ball at Tyrone, Tyrone couldn't take it anymore. "Dillon!" he exclaimed. "Quit farting around!"

Was Dillon passing gas on top of avoiding his work? No. **Farting around just means you're wasting time.** It's a way of saying that someone isn't doing what they're supposed to be doing.

How did *farting around* come to mean that someone's doing pointless things? The story behind this phrase is a little murky. Most people think it's just a funny takeoff on phrases such as *goofing around* and *messing around.*

What we know for sure is that phrases related to farting have been around for a long time. That could be because lots of people think farting is kind of funny—so phrases that use the word *fart* have long been popular. Even the writer Geoffrey Chaucer included some funny lines involving farting in his fourteenth-century work *The Canterbury Tales.*

Geoffrey Chaucer might look serious, but he thought farting was funny. No joke!

If you're making paper airplanes instead of focusing on science, you might say that you're farting around.

Wherever the phrase comes from, just make sure that *you* don't get caught farting around when you should be focusing on science. Of course, if you do, you could always say that you're conducting an experiment in doing nothing while you should be doing something. Think your teacher would buy that one?

ALL POOPED OUT

Aiko spent the day cleaning her room, and she told her mom at dinner that she was all pooped out.

Sounds like Aiko has a really messy and stinky problem. She should probably stay in the bathroom until she's better, right? Not quite. Aiko is just tired, that's all. **Being pooped out means you are exhausted and need some time to rest.**

The word *poop* has been around for centuries. It comes from the Latin word *puppis*. This word described the stern, or the rear end, of a ship. By the 1700s, people were calling that part of a ship the poop deck.

Poop also happens to be a word for excrement—which is a fancy term for the stuff you put in the toilet. And no, we don't mean your sister's toothbrush. Poop is the by-product, or waste, left over from what you eat. (Hey, it may be gross, but it's got to go somewhere!)

Should you stay close to one of these if you're all pooped out? No! Pooped out means you're tired. It doesn't mean you have to . . . you know.

So when we use the phrase "all pooped out," are we referring to the back end of a ship…or to the contents of a toilet? Neither one, as it turns out! Most people think we use this phrase because the word *pooped* sounds similar to the sound you might make when you are totally exhausted. Try it—inhale deeply and whisper *poooooop.* Just try not to do it in the library. The librarian probably won't be amused.

Here's the poop deck! It has nothing to do with the contents of a toilet.

SNOT-NOSED BRAT

Ava's little brother keeps sneaking into her room and taking things that don't belong to him. First, he grabbed her Pillow Pet. Then he ran away with a board game she'd set out to play with her friends at a sleepover tonight.

Ava had finally had enough. "Get out of here, you snot-nosed brat!" she shouts the next time she sees him lurking in the hallway.

Does Ava's brother have snot dripping from his nose? Well, sometimes he does—especially during cold and flu season. But Ava doesn't actually mean to say that her brother's nose is full of snot. **What she means is that her brother is acting in a super obnoxious way.**

When someone accuses another person of being a snot-nosed brat, it means that the accuser thinks the person's acting thoughtlessly. A snot-nosed brat doesn't seem to care too much about other people's feelings.

So how did having a snotty nose come to be connected with being thoughtless? It may be because when your nose is clogged with snot, your voice usually sounds a little nasally. And there's a stereotype out there that says conceited people talk in nasally voices.

Now, don't get us wrong: it's OK to have a nasally voice sometimes. Snotty noses are OK too. They may even be unavoidable in the winter, when everyone seems to have one. Just try not to act like a snot-nosed brat. Your family and friends will definitely appreciate it.

Brothers...you gotta love 'em. Or not!

MAKING a STINK

Robbie is upset that he has to clear the table. "It isn't faaaair!" he cries. "I don't wanna clear the table! I wanna go play Xbox!"

"Robbie," his dad says in a warning voice. "You know the rules. No playing Xbox until after you've put the dishes in the dishwasher. Now quit making a stink about it, and please just finish the job."

Does Robbie's dad really think he stinks? Does Robbie have a body-odor problem? No! Robbie is just annoyed, and he's saying and doing things that are not helpful. **That's what making a stink means.**

Why do we say that someone's making a stink when he or she is behaving badly? It's probably because when something stinks, it obviously isn't very pleasant. Just think about your brother's unwashed socks in the hamper down the hall or steaming fish sticks from the school lunchroom. You don't want to spend a lot of time breathing in *those* odors, do you?

Don't make a stink when your mom or dad asks you to clean up. It's better to stay cheerful and get the work done fast. Then you can move on to something fun!

It's kind of the same thing with bad behavior. <u>You don't want to spend a ton of time around someone who's whining or overreacting.</u>

So the next time you get a bad report card or your sister eats the last cupcake, remember Robbie's father's warning about not making a stink. Try not to get too upset, and stop and think before you act. After all, you don't want people running away from you the way they would from stinky fish sticks, do you?

By the SKIN of YOUR TEETH

Meredith passed the social studies pop quiz by the skin of her teeth.

Since when do teeth have skin? Is Meredith some kind of weird-looking alien? Or maybe she doesn't brush her teeth too often. Ew! **Nah, *by the skin of her teeth* just means she barely passed her quiz.** People use this phrase in all kinds of situations where they just barely manag e to do something.

The saying *by the skin of your teeth* has been around for a long time. In fact, it's as old as the Bible! There's a passage in the Bible's book of Job that talks about Job escaping by the skin of his teeth.

Teeth definitely don't have skin ... so what gives?

But what does skin on teeth have to do with escaping? Well, *skin* in this case may not really mean skin, as in the stuff that covers your body. Skin just might mean the outer surface of your teeth. And since teeth aren't very big, they have a pretty small surface. So that's why escaping by the skin of your teeth means escaping by a small or narrow margin.

Of course, it's usually better to escape a bad fate easily rather than by the skin of your teeth—right? So maybe you'll want to crack the books tonight instead of playing video games. After all, you never know when *your* teacher might surprise you with a pop quiz!

Crack those books and you'll pass your tests by more than the skin of your teeth!

FOAMING at the MOUTH

Enrique really wants to see the new movie that was advertised on TV the other day. "When I saw the commercial for *Super Crazy Aliens Chasing Cars*, I was foaming at the mouth!" he tells his friend Matt at recess.

Did the commercial actually make Enrique's mouth foam? Is this kid turning into a wild dog or what? Nope. Matt doesn't have to worry. As Enrique explains, "I just can't wait to see the movie. It's going to be so awesome!" **That's all *foaming at the mouth* means—that you're super excited about something.**

Why do people say they're foaming at the mouth when they just mean they're really excited? It's because dogs and other animals whose emotions are out of control sometimes do foam at the mouth—especially when they have an illness called rabies. Rabies is a disease of the nervous system. It causes animals to lose control of themselves. They sometimes display extreme rage and hypersalivate (a fancy term for foaming at the mouth).

If people tell you that they're foaming at the mouth, don't start looking for drool on their faces. Don't assume that they have rabies either. Instead, know that they're just really excited about something—just like Enrique is to see those crazy aliens.

This guy's super excited about the trophy he just won. You might even say he's foaming at the mouth.

SOMETHING SMELLS FISHY

Danny looked over the baseball cards he'd just gotten in a trade he made with the new kid down the street. Now that he thinks about it, the cards don't seem as good as the old cards he just left with his neighbor. "Something smells fishy," Danny mutters to himself.

What's the deal? Do Danny's baseball cards smell like fish? Or maybe his mom is cooking cod for dinner, and the smell is wafting all the way down the block. Nah. **Danny just didn't feel like things were right. That's what people mean when they say something smells fishy.**

What does smelling fishy have to do with something feeling suspicious? Are we saying that fish are dishonest? Are they hiding something underneath those scales?

No, fish are perfectly respectable creatures. It's just that they can be a little slippery. Ever tried to hold a fish that someone caught in a lake or in the ocean? It isn't easy. _Slippery can also be a word to describe_

This fish market smells fishy for real! But that icky fishy scent isn't what people are talking about when they say something smells fishy.

someone who's <u>dishonest.</u> So when we say that something or someone smells fishy, we're saying that the thing or person seems slippery like a fish. Fish can also have a bad odor. Most people don't like

I smell a rat is another common phrase people use when something seems suspicious.

things that stink. And they don't like suspicious people or situations either. That's another reason people say a suspicious situation smells fishy.

Sometimes we use the saying "I smell a rat" when something doesn't seem right. It basically means the same thing as "something smells fishy." Rats may not be slippery, but they do spend a lot of time in garbage cans. And all that exposure to garbage means that rats probably don't smell any better than fish.

Whether someone says a situation smells like a fish or like a rat, you're probably better off proceeding with caution. Otherwise, you may end up like Danny: stuck in a position that you'd rather not be in.

FLESH and BLOOD

Cami hated how her older sister teased her so much. Today she called Cami a baby just because she'd cried a little after falling off her bike. "That's no way to treat your own flesh and blood," Cami told her sister.

Flesh and blood? Ew! What's Cami talking about? It sounds like she's at a meat counter in the local grocery store. Of course, she's not. **Flesh and blood just refers to someone you're related to.** A sister or a parent might be your flesh and blood.

There's plenty of flesh in this butcher shop. But this kind of flesh has nothing to do with the saying *flesh and blood!*

Why is someone you're related to called your flesh and blood? It's because people who are related share some physical things in common. For example, you and your brother might have the same color hair. Or you and your mom might both have freckles and wear glasses.

You could even say that you and the people you're related to have the same flesh on your bodies and blood in your veins—which is exactly where this expression comes from.

So the next time you hear the saying *flesh and blood*, don't be alarmed. No one's talking about a side of cow hanging up at a meat counter. They're just talking about people who happen to be related. Unless, of course, you're speaking to a butcher.

This brother and sister have the same color hair. They are related by flesh and blood.

You ARE What You EAT

Mandy ate a forkful of her chocolate cake before she'd even touched her veggies. "Mandy, take a bite or two of your peas, please," said her mom. "You may have dessert after you've eaten more of your dinner. After all, you are what you eat!"

Is Mandy turning into chocolate cake? Worse things could happen, right? She *could* turn into a big pile of peas—which is what her mom wants her to eat. But Mandy isn't turning into either chocolate cake or peas. **You are what you eat just means that what you eat helps determine how healthy you will be.**

Your next school photo just may look like this if you eat lots of chocolate cake. (Just kidding.)

Sweet fruit is a tasty treat that's also good for you!

The saying *you are what you eat* dates back to the early 1800s. The point of the saying was to make people think a little harder about the things they ate. Parents and teachers often still use the saying to remind kids that a balanced diet is good. One can't live on chocolate cake alone!

The next time you eat a plateful of broccoli, run to the mirror and check things out. Is your hair getting kind of bushy? Is your skin turning green? Of course not. See? Don't take the saying literally. But if you *are* looking greenish, you could always try eating a big bowl of fruit.

BITE Your TONGUE!

"Bite your tongue!" whispered Sandeep's older sister as Sandeep began talking about the surprise birthday party for their grandpa.

Does Sandeep's sister really want him to bite his tongue? Ouch! That probably wouldn't feel very good. Why would his sister tell him to do that? Well, she doesn't really mean that he should chomp down on his tongue. **She just means that he needs to keep quiet about a surprise.** After all, their grandpa's sitting right across from them at the dinner table.

If you start to get a little bit too chatty, someone might tell you to bite your tongue.

The saying *bite your tongue* has been around since the late 1500s. You can probably guess where it comes from. If you bite your tongue, it wouldn't be too easy to talk. And putting a stop to talking is exactly what people are trying to do if they tell you to bite your tongue.

So if you're ever gabbing away about something that's supposed to be a secret or telling a friend a rumor that you probably shouldn't be spreading, don't be surprised if someone asks you to bite your tongue. And if someone does, you could even try gently securing your teeth around your tongue to keep yourself from saying too much! Then you might try sputtering out, "I'm thorry for thawking!"

Don't go spreading rumors that you really shouldn't be spreading!

COUGHING UP a LUNG

Curtis has had a hacking cough for a week now. He always gets this way when allergy season starts. When he was watching TV with his family last night, he had an especially bad coughing episode. "Curtis, dude," said his brother. "You're coughing up a lung!"

What did Curtis's brother mean? Could Curtis actually cough up one of his lungs? Gross!

Of course he couldn't. **The saying *coughing up a lung* just means that you are doing some serious coughing.** And Curtis certainly was!

While you can't cough up a lung, it *is* possible to spit out other stuff when you cough.

Ugh! This kid has a killer cough that just keeps hanging on.

That stuff could include saliva, mucus, and sputum—a thick, sticky liquid that our bodies sometimes make when we're sick.

Curtis isn't sick, so he's not coughing up sputum. But if it ever happens to you—or if you ever have unexplained coughing that just won't go away—you should probably see a doctor. You might have the flu or an infection.

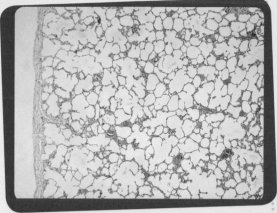

This close-up photo shows what lung tissue looks like. Don't worry—you won't cough it up, even if you feel like you're coughing up a lung.

In very rare cases, bad coughing can be a sign of a more serious problem. Lung diseases can cause extremely severe coughing. One form of lung disease is pneumonoultramicroscopicsilicovolcanoconeosis. Yes, this is a real word—and it happens to be one of the longest words in the dictionary!

Fortunately, this disease doesn't affect kids. The only way you can get it is by breathing in tiny particles of silica (a chemical compound often used to make glass). This means that you'll never have to worry about telling your teacher that you missed class because of pneumonoultramicroscopicsilicovolcanoconeosis!

Glossary

emesis: the scientific term for vomiting

excrement: the waste material left over from what you eat

hematidrosis: the scientific term for sweating blood

hypersalivate: to drool excessively

idiom: a commonly used expression or phrase that means something different from what it appears to mean

pneumonoultramicroscopicsilicovolcanoconeosis: a lung disease caused by inhaling tiny particles of silica, a chemical compound often used to make glass

rabies: a disease of the nervous system that causes warm-blooded animals to lose control of themselves. Rabies is caused by a virus that attacks the brain and spinal cord and is spread by the bite of an infected animal.

sputum: a thick, sticky liquid that our bodies sometimes make when we're sick

Further Reading

Behnke, Alison. *Can Rats Swim from Sewers into Toilets? And Other Questions about Your Home.* Minneapolis: Lerner Publications Company, 2011. Find out the truth behind several fun, funny, and gross beliefs and sayings about that place where we spend most of our time—home.

Doeden, Matt. *Stick Out Like a Sore Thumb: And Other Expressions about Body Parts.* Minneapolis: Lerner Publications Company, 2013. Explore the meaning and origin of expressions such as *stick out like a sore thumb, by a nose, and pulling your leg.*

Donovan, Sandy. *Rumble & Spew: Gross Stuff in Your Stomach and Intestines.* Minneapolis: Millbrook Press, 2010. If you like gross-out books, you'll love this icky and interesting look at the digestive system.

Idioms by Kids
http://www.idiomsbykids.com
Check out more than one thousand kid-drawn pictures of the literal meanings of idioms. You can add your own examples too.

Idiom Site
http://www.idiomsite.com
Visit this website for an alphabetical list of expressions and what they mean.

KidsHealth: Kids' Talk
http://kidshealth.org/kid/talk
This health site for kids includes a section all about expressions. Click on the link called Where's That Come From? to get the story on expressions ranging from *butterflies in the stomach* to *have your heart in your mouth.*

Klingel, Cynthia. *Ack! There's a Bug in My Ear! (And Other Sayings That Just Aren't True).* Mankato, MN: Child's World, 2008. Discover the meaning behind some of the world's strangest expressions, including *put a bug in one's ear.*

Moses, Will. *Raining Cats & Dogs.* New York: Philomel Books, 2008. Entertaining text and whimsical art help explain some common but puzzling sayings.

Paint by Idioms
http://www.funbrain.com/funbrain/idioms
Test your knowledge of common idioms by taking the multiple-choice quizzes on this site from FunBrain.

LERNER
SOURCE™
Expand learning beyond the printed book. Download free, complementary educational resources for this book from our website, www.lernerresource.com.

Index

Photo Acknowledgments

The images in this book are used with the permission of: © Rob Melnychuk/Brand X Pictures/Getty Images, p. 5; © Miradrozdowski/Dreamstime.com, p. 6; © Phanie/SuperStock, p. 7; © Stock Montage/Archive Photos/Getty Images, p. 8; © Zoran Milich/Photonica/Getty Images, p. 9; © iStockphoto.com/RonTech2000, p. 10; © Jason Edwards/National Geographic/Getty Images, p. 11; © Alders Photography/Flickr/Getty Images, p. 13; © Gemenacom/Dreamstime.com, p. 14; © Kin Images/Photographer's Choice RF/Getty Images, p. 16; © Jupiterimages/Workbook Stock/Getty Images, p. 17; © Jasper Cole/Blend Images/Getty Images, p. 19; © Mikael Damkier/Dreamstime.com, p. 20; © age fotostock/SuperStock, p. 21; © Lyn Baxter/Dreamstime.com, p. 22; © Jacek Chabraszewski/Dreamstime.com, p. 23; © Lisa F. Young/Dreamstime.com, p. 24; © Markstout/Dreamstime.com, p. 25; © Dennie Cody/Workbook Stock/Getty Images, p. 26; © Laurent Renault/Dreamstime.com, p. 27; © Joruba/Dreamstime.com, p. 28; © Biophoto Associates/Photo Researchers, Inc, p. 29.

Front cover: © Martin Williams/Alamy (main); © iStockphoto.com/Lior Filshteiner (toilet paper).

Main body text set in Adrianna Light 11/17.
Typeface provided by Chank.